LIFE in the Future

SPACE EXPLORATION

Mark Beyer

HIGH
interest

books

Children's Press®

A
New York / ~~~~~~~~~~~~ d / Sydney
Mexico City / New Delhi / Hong Kong
Danbury, Connecticut

Book Design: Christopher Logan
Contributing Editor: Scott Waldman

Photo Credits: pp. Cover, 7, 8, 13, 14, 15, 16, 19, 22, 23, 24, 28, 31, 32 © NASA;
pp. 4, 21 © Corbis; p. 18 © Bettmann/Corbis; p. 26 © AFP/Corbis;
p. 34 © PhotoDisc; p. 37 © Pat Rawlings; p. 41 © Roger Ressmeyer/Corbis

Library of Congress Cataloging-in-Publication Data

Beyer, Mark (Mark T.)
Space exploration / by Mark Beyer.
    v. cm. -- (Life in the future)
Includes index.
Contents: Bringing people into space, rocket engines and ships -- Earth
orbit telescopes -- Living in space, the International Space Station --
Our future in space, Moon colonies and Mars missions.
ISBN 0-516-23917-1 (lib. bdg.) -- ISBN 0-516-24008-0 (pbk.)
1. Astronautics--Juvenile literature. 2. Outer
space--Exploration--Juvenile literature. 3. Space colonies--Juvenile
literature. [1. Astronautics. 2. Outer space--Exploration. 3. Space
colonies.] I. Title. II. Series.
TL793 .B446 2002
629.4--dc21

                                2002002871

CONTENTS

H.G. Wells may have dreamed that people would someday walk on the Moon, but he died twenty-three years before it ever happened.

People laughed at writer H.G. Wells when he wrote a book about space travel called *The First Men in the Moon* in 1901. At the time walking on the Moon was a ridiculous idea to most people. But Wells had the last laugh. Sixty-eight years after he wrote his book, two American astronauts *did* travel through space and walk on the Moon. They used a spacecraft that traveled faster and farther than anyone—including Wells— could have imagined.

A hundred years ago, people only dreamed of going to the Moon. Today, we can say our astronauts have already been there. Now their sights are set on Mars. Early manned rockets could take only one person into space and could not be used a second time. Today, the space shuttle carries up to seven astronauts into space and can be reused many times.

Living in space is no longer a fictional idea from books and movies. The International Space Station (ISS) is already up and running. The ISS is a laboratory and living quarters for astronauts that orbits Earth. In the years to come, as parts are added, it will grow in size and use.

In the near future, we will see many exciting new developments in space exploration. Projects are underway for new space rockets and space vehicles. A new rover mission to Mars is also being planned. Soon, we could even see a colony of people living and working on the Moon. The dreams of H.G. Wells's time are becoming the realities of today and tomorrow.

⬤ *This picture is taken from the space shuttle* Endeavor *as it approaches* Zarya, *one of the parts of the International Space Station.*

The space shuttle Atlantis *blasts off into space with its rocket engines. The engines will come off and fall back to Earth when the shuttle is in space.*

CHAPTER ONE

SPACE TRAVEL

The space shuttle, satellites, and space station parts all have to be sent into space. Getting them into space is one of the greatest challenges in space exploration. The shuttle carries satellites and all of the ISS parts into orbit, but the shuttle itself must be launched into space. The space shuttle uses rockets to lift off into the darkness of space.

Rocket engines work by turning flammable fuels, which burn easily, into hot gases. The fuel used in rocket engines is a mixture of liquid oxygen and liquid nitrogen. These fuels are mixed in a chamber where they burn. This creates a gas, which is forced through a nozzle. The flaming gases fire from the open ends of the nozzle

TECH TALK

Environmentally Safe Rocket Fuels

Liquid oxygen and liquid hydrogen are highly flammable when mixed. They burn hot enough to lift a rocket into space, yet their exhaust is nothing but steam! Steam does not harm our environment. Hopefully, scientists will invent a safe way to use oxygen and hydrogen to power our cars. As a result, car emissions would no longer pollute Earth's air.

creating a powerful thrust. This thrust propels the rocket and all of it's weight into space at speeds of 5,000 to 10,000 miles per hour (8,047 to 16,093 kilometers per hour).

SAFETY IN SPACE

Space is the last great frontier for people to explore, but space can be a dangerous place to work. One of the most important aspects of space exploration is safety. When things go wrong, it is very difficult to rescue scientists who work in space. For example, what would happen to the scientists on the ISS if there were an emergency? Without a plan for escape, they would probably die. New vehicles are being developed that will allow scientists to return safely to Earth in case of danger. The X-38 is one example.

THE X-38 RESCUE VEHICLE

Even if the space shuttle were sitting on its launch pad, it would take hours to reach astronauts or scientists on the ISS. Such an emergency has been on space engineers' minds for many decades. What they needed was some sort of lifeboat. Enter the X-38.

The National Aeronautics and Space Administration (NASA) has been developing a rescue vehicle for use on space stations since the 1970s. Tests have helped NASA engineers develop a small, durable ship capable of rescuing a crew of seven. The X-38 will be a vehicle that can sit around unused for years and still be ready to take off on a moment's notice.

In creating the X-38, engineers used electric motors for power, and the Global Positioning System (GPS) for navigation. A wedge-shaped body was designed so the vehicle could fly without wings. A huge parafoil, or parachute, was constructed for an easy, safe landing.

During an emergency, such as illness or mechanical failure, the crew on the ISS can undock the X-38 in less than 3 minutes. Then, they can fire its engine and descend toward Earth. This rescue vehicle can be flown by the ground control crew on Earth. The crew on board can also fly the X-38 themselves. Once in Earth's atmosphere, the X-38 will glide toward the ground. At 23,000 feet (7,010 meters), the huge parafoil opens. The crew can steer the parafoil. The ship will land on skids instead of wheels. Skids are flat pieces of metal that can glide easier over rocky ground than wheels can. This will allow the X-38 to land on rough ground.

● *The X-38 rescue vehicle can be ready for life-saving action in less than 3 minutes.*

It wasn't until 2000
that a crew was able to
live on board the ISS.

In 2003, NASA plans to send the X-38 to the ISS aboard the space shuttle. This life-saving spacecraft will be an important part of space exploration in the future.

Astronauts Daniel W. Bursch (left), Yuri I. Onufrienko (center), and Carl E. Walz (right) pose for a photo aboard the ISS in December 2001.

When the Hubble Space Telescope is being repaired, it is attached to the space shuttle.

CHAPTER TWO

EARTH-ORBIT TELESCOPES

Future space exploration is not only about flying spaceships into orbit. It goes even further than building space stations or thinking about colonizing the moon. All future space exploration begins with an observation of our solar system. Scientists observe space by looking through telescopes that orbit Earth.

The Hubble Space Telescope (HST) has been orbiting Earth since April 1990. Since that time, HST has been sending thousands of photographs of our solar system, our galaxy, and the universe back to Earth. The HST project is run by NASA and the European Space Agency (ESA).

At 380 miles (612 km) above Earth, the HST is truly a window to the galaxies. The amount of light it can see coming from great distances is ten

The Hubble Space Telescope was named after famed American astronomer Edwin P. Hubble.

times greater than that of Earth-based telescopes. The HST is able to view celestial bodies, like moons, stars, suns, and planets, from hundreds of millions of light years away. A light year is the distance light travels in one year. Light travels at 186,282 miles (299,792 km) per second. The HST has actually performed much better than any astronomer could have imagined.

How the HST Works

The Hubble's main observatory mirror is 8 feet (2.4 m) in diameter. Its other instruments include three cameras and guidance sensors. The cameras

The Hubble Space Telescope has been able to work in space for so long by collecting the rays of the Sun in its solar arrays and converting them to power.

capture light in different ways. One camera takes wide-angle photographs of celestial bodies. Another camera takes infrared photos. Infrared light is invisible to the unaided eye. These cameras capture light otherwise invisible to the observatory mirror. The third camera is the Faint Object Camera (FOC), built by the ESA.

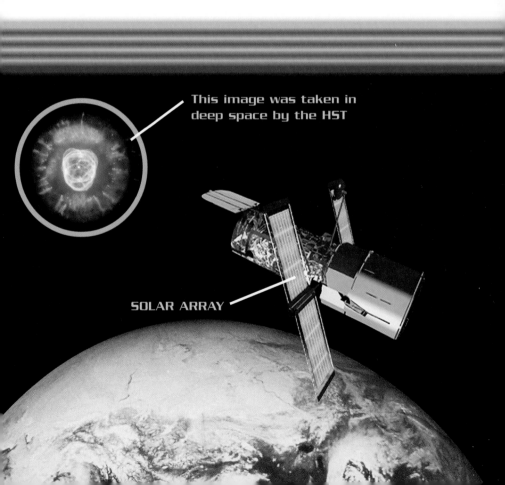

This image was taken in deep space by the HST

SOLAR ARRAY

The FOC expands images by increasing the light hitting the observatory mirror by more than 100,000 times. The guidance sensors help steer the mirror toward specific points in space. All of these operations of the HST are controlled from Earth.

What We Learn from HST

The images that the HST records can help us understand how the universe was formed. This high-powered telescope has photographed gases flowing around celestial bodies. These pictures can help us understand how a planet's atmosphere is made. The HST has also photographed light and colors surrounding stars. This information helps us learn about our own Sun's formation, history, and future.

SPACE TELESCOPE FUTURE: THE NGST

As early as 2009, the Next Generation Space Telescope (NGST) will be launched. The NGST will be sent into orbit 940,000 miles (1,512,786 km)

Louis Lagrange was a French mathematician and physicist. In the nineteenth century, he discovered that there were many orbital positions in our solar system. Orbital positions are the points in the universe where an object will stay in orbit around a particular planet. Today we call these positions Lagrange points.

from Earth. This distance is known as L2, or the second Lagrange point. L2 is two times farther from Earth than the Moon is. Once the NGST is set in this position, it will orbit at that distance forever. The NGST will provide scientists with a view of the universe even better than the HST has given them.

NGST Instruments and Use

Much of the infrared light coming from deep space is blocked from telescopes on Earth, and even the HST, by interstellar gas and dust.

Being so far out into space will let the NGST see objects and light 100 to 1,000 times darker than any that have previously been seen. The NGST's cameras will be able to pick up infrared light coming from distant galaxies and solar systems. Computers will map the light to create an image for scientists to look at.

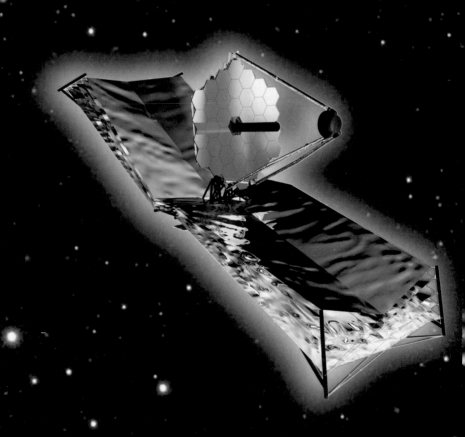

Scientists are still not certain what the Next Generation Space Telescope will look like. These are two possible designs for the NGST.

CHAPTER THREE

LIVING IN SPACE

In 1984, President Ronald Reagan announced that NASA would build a space station. Fifteen other countries joined the United States to share costs and help develop the project. These countries are Russia, Japan, Canada, Italy, Belgium, the Netherlands, Denmark, Norway, France, Spain, Germany, Sweden, Switzerland, the United Kingdom, and Brazil.

In 1998, the first part of the International Space Station was launched into space. It was called *Zarya*, which means "sunrise" in the Russian language. It was designed to be the main power source for the ISS. Since then, ten missions by Russian rockets and United States' space shuttles have taken place. These missions have brought new pieces of equipment and working and living modules into orbit.

This illustration shows what the International Space Station will look like when it is completed.

By 2004, the ISS will have six science labs attached to its main frame. Forty-five missions will have been flown to bring everything up into space. Almost 500 tons of equipment, supplies, and modules will orbit around Earth. The ISS will measure 290 feet (88 m) long and 356 feet (109 m) wide. It will have a living and workspace equal to the insides of two Boeing 747 jets. Right now, a permanent crew of three lives on the ISS. In the future, a permanent crew of six or seven will occupy the ISS.

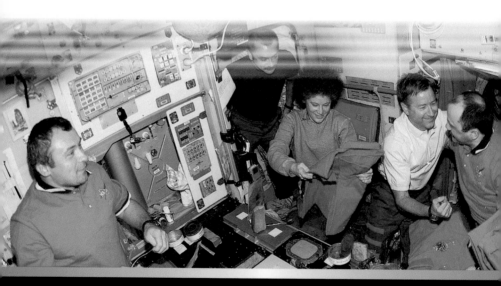

Living and working quarters are a bit tight on the ISS. But this joint effort of sixteen countries will tell us much about life in space.

LIFE SYSTEMS IN SPACE

To live in space, people need the same things that they do on Earth: air, water, food, heat, and shelter. The power supply for the ISS comes from solar power and batteries. Arrays, or solar panels, capture the Sun's heat. This heat is converted into electric power. Some of it is stored in batteries. The array wings of the ISS are more than 108 feet (33 m) long.

The electricity heats the ISS and runs a system that cleans the drinking water. The ISS orbits Earth every 90 minutes. During this time the Sun is shadowed behind Earth for 30 minutes. Battery power takes over while the ISS passes behind Earth.

● TECH TALK

The International Space Station orbits Earth at 17,500 miles (28,164 km) per hour! It is 220 miles (354 km) from Earth.

Science Labs

The United States owns one of the six science labs attached to the ISS. Its name is Destiny. It was brought to the ISS in February 2001 on the shuttle *Atlantis*. Destiny is 28 feet (8.5 m) long and 14 feet (4.3 m) wide and is made of light-weight aluminum. It is wrapped in insulation. In space, insulation is needed to protect structures from harsh temperatures. Kevlar, which is used in bulletproof vests, covers the insulation. This outer layer of Kevlar protects Destiny from damage caused by flying space junk and tiny meteoroids.

Destiny has its own power source supplied by solar arrays. The temperature inside Destiny is controlled. A crew of three or four can work in

Destiny is protected against tiny meteoroids, which can put holes in spacecraft.

total comfort. The crew's sleeping quarters are the largest ever available to astronaut scientists. The crew members will drink water purer than water in most cities in the United States. Destiny has a window from which scientists can look at Earth. Viewing our planet as the ISS orbits will make the scientists working in Destiny feel closer to home.

SCIENCE GAINS

The ISS is an ideal environment for scientific study and observation. The ISS allows scientists to get a closer view of the solar system while they are studying it.

Life Science

The ISS life-science researchers will focus on many subjects. One of the missions of the ISS is to study how outer space affects the human body. Scientists will study how the body and mind adapt to long periods in space. We already know that muscles break down in space and bones lose their density. Scientists are trying to find ways to prevent this from happening. Understanding these challenges will help long-distance space travelers adjust to being away from Earth for an extended time.

Scientists want to see how other life forms react to space, too. The ISS will have facilities to grow cells and tissue cultures. Scientists will raise plants, insects, rodents, marine life, birds, and reptiles. Learning how other life forms react to living in space will give us a better understanding of basic biology and what the future of living in space may hold for humans.

Space Science

The ISS will greatly improve the study of our solar system. Scientists on board the ISS plan to study solar winds, planetary weather, and asteroids. Each can tell us a great deal about Earth, and life on Earth. For example, scientists plan on studying the Sun to see if it has anything to do with Earth's global warming problem.

Global warming is the heating up of Earth's surface. Many scientists think it is caused by sunspot activity on the Sun. Sunspots are dark spots on the Sun that are not as hot as the area surrounding them. They give off huge amounts of radiation. The radiation heat travels to Earth on solar winds. By studying sunspot activity, scientists can perhaps better understand how to combat global warming.

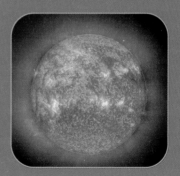

Understanding sunspots may someday help scientists figure out patterns of global warming.

Buzz Aldrin (above) and Neil Armstrong were the first two people ever to set foot on the Moon.

CHAPTER FOUR

OUR FUTURE IN SPACE

In 1969, the astronauts on Apollo 11 returned from their Moon landing with samples of rocks and dirt. Other Moon-landing missions collected hundreds of pounds of Moon rocks. Scientists have found that the Moon contains some elements that are also found on Earth. This discovery has given scientists hope that Moon colonies can be built to support human life. If scientists can build a base on the Moon, the future of space exploration will change.

Why bother living on the Moon at all? Like the ISS, the Moon would be a perfect place for scientists to live and work. Studying space, our solar system, and how humans may adapt to live in space will increase our understanding of the universe. Results of studying the Moon show that living on it may be quite possible.

ELEMENT-RICH MOON

Moon ores have proven to contain:

- Oxygen
- Silicon
- Aluminum
- Iron
- Titanium
- Magnesium
- Hydrogen
- Helium

Life-Support Needs

Moon soil contains two elements critical to human life—oxygen and hydrogen. It also has Helium-3, silicon, and the metals aluminum, titanium, iron, and magnesium. Each of these elements will be useful to supporting human life on the Moon.

Oxygen is also found in another substance we need to live—water. A machine can connect oxygen and hydrogen atoms taken from Moon soil to create water. There is also water on the

Moon, in the form of ice. Where did this water come from? We know that comets contain ice. So it is possible that water found on the Moon could have come from comets that hit it millions of years ago.

Oxygen can also be used to make rocket fuel. This would make the Moon a perfect place to begin space missions. Helium-3 can be used for fusion reactors. These reactors are used to make electric power. Silicon is used to make glass and solar cells. These cells would be used for energy collection. The metals can be used to make parts for buildings in which people can live. Much of what is needed to live on the Moon is already found on it!

TECH TALK

People living in moon colonies will grow their own food. Rice, fruit, vegetables, and other foods will be grown in climate-controlled domes. Foods have been successfully grown in similar space-like domes on Earth. Biosphere 2, built in Arizona, was one such project.

Structures

The Moon has only one-sixth the gravity of Earth. A person weighing 180 pounds (82 kilograms) on Earth weighs only 30 pounds (14 kg) on the Moon. This is because there is less gravity on the Moon. Since there is less gravity and no wind on the Moon, structures can be built taller than Earth-based buildings.

SPACE OBSERVATIONS

Telescopes

The Moon does not have an atmosphere. This would give Moon-based telescopes very clear visibility. No dust or radiation will interfere as it does in Earth's atmosphere.

The HST uses expensive equipment to point the telescope in the right direction. So will the future NGST orbiters. Telescopes operating on the Moon won't need this type of equipment, reducing costs and saving time! Telescopes on the Moon can also be used at any time while Earth-based telescopes can only be used at

A computer-generated image shows what a future Moon colony might look like.

night. Telescopes can be mounted behind hills that block the Sun's rays and earthlight. Shaded telescopes see deeper into dark space without interference from sunlight.

Earth Study

The Moon is also the best place from which to study our planet. From the Moon almost half of Earth can be seen at once. As Earth turns, scientists on the Moon will be able to study weather, and tidal and ocean currents.

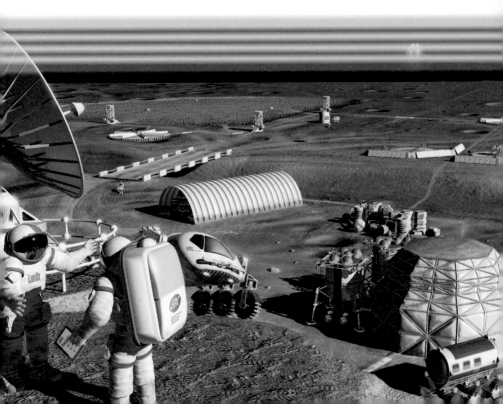

MISSIONS TO MARS

NASA and the ESA have already studied Mars from up close. Orbiting satellites have given us information about the Martian atmosphere. We've learned that there is water on the "Red Planet." In 1997, the *Mars Pathfinder* landed on Mars. This mission was able to send out a rover onto the surface of Mars. A rover is small vehicle capable of moving on the ground. It can be controlled from Earth. The rover explored a small area and gave scientists data about Martian atmosphere and geology. The success of this mission set the stage for another robot rover mission to Mars's surface.

The 2001 Mars Odyssey

The *2001 Mars Odyssey* was launched in April 2001. It began orbiting Mars on October 24, 2001. *Odyssey* may tell scientists for the first time many facts about the Martian atmosphere.

Three Instruments Will Take Measurements on Mars

Thermal Emission Imaging System (THEMIS)
THEMIS measures the amount of minerals that may be present on Mars. Scientists are especially interested in minerals that only water helps create.

Gamma Ray Spectrometer (GRS) This instrument will tell scientists if any chemical elements are on Mars's surface. GRS can measure up to twenty elements.

Mars Radiation Environment Experiment (MARIE)
MARIE measures the level of radiation on Mars. This is important for future planned human exploration of Mars.

THE MARS EXPLORATION ROVERS (MER)

The MER mission is set to launch between May and July 2003. A parachute and airbags will help two MERs land softly on Mars in January or February 2004. The two rovers will then move out and explore the Martian surface. These rovers are much larger and more powerful than the Pathfinder rover.

Instruments will gather data about Martian soil. Cameras will photograph rocks and other formations. A rock abrasion tool (RAT) will scrape Martian rocks for samples. Scientists hope to find more elements and chemicals under rock surfaces using RAT. The two 300-pound (136 kg) rovers should work until May 2004.

THE (DISTANT) FUTURE OF SPACE EXPLORATION

People have been studying space for thousands of years. Only now are we on the edge of making discoveries beyond our wildest dreams. Even as you read this, space probes are reaching

TECH TALK

The best time to send a spacecraft to Mars happens only once every twenty-six months. This is when Mars and Earth are closest to each other in their orbits around the Sun. Spacecraft can use the least amount of fuel for the six-and-a-half-month trip.

farther into deep space—visiting uncharted territories, making new discoveries, and transmitting important data back to Earth. The future of space exploration travels with them. Each day we gain new insight into our universe.

Only our imaginations and the new technology we develop can limit what we learn and where we go. The future of space exploration can be as boundless as space itself.

atmosphere a planet's air

celestial bodies things in space, such as moons, comets, planets, and stars

efficient being productive without wasting time or energy

engineers people who design and make machines, vehicles, bridges, or roads

exhaust the waste gas produced by a vehicle's engine

flammable capable of igniting easily and burning quickly

global positioning system (GPS) a device that tells a person where he or she is

infrared light that cannot be seen by the human eye

light year the distance light travels in one year, 5.88 trillion miles (9.46 trillion km)

module an independently-operable unit that is part of a larger space vehicle

orbit to move around something at the same distance each time

parafoil a large parachute that opens up to slow down a spacecraft when it falls to Earth

resistance the force put against a moving object by wind, water, or gravity

satellites objects, such as a moon or spacecraft, that orbit around a planet

service module the part of a space vehicle station that powers the structure

solar arrays solar energy panels that capture the Sun's heat to make it into electricity

FOR FURTHER READING

Desomma, Vincent V. *The Mission to Mars and Beyond.* New York, NY: Chelsea House, 1992.

Hamilton, John. *Future Missions to Mars.* Edina, MN: ABDO Publishing, 1998.

Paul, Richard. *A Handbook to the Universe: Explorations of Matter, Energy, Space, and Time for Beginning Scientific Thinkers.* Chicago, IL: Chicago Review Press, 1993.

Sipiera, Diane M., and Paul P. Sipiera. *Space Stations.* Danbury, CT: Grolier Publishing, 1998.

Stott, Carole, and Steve Gorton. *Space Exploration.* New York, NY: DK Publishing, 2000.

Organizations

The Mars Society
P.O. Box 273
Indian Hills, CO 80454
www.marssociety.org
This group seeks to educate youth about Mars
and space exploration.

Students for the Education and Development
of Space (SEDS)
SEDS-USA
MIT Room W20-445
77 Massachusetts Avenue
Cambridge, MA 02139-4307
1-888-321-SEDS
http://seds.lpl.arizona.edu/seds/
SEDS is an organization run by students with
the goal of getting young people interested in
space exploration.

RESOURCES

Web Sites

2001 Mars Odyssey

http://mars.jpl.nasa.gov/odyssey/mission/index.html
Visit this site to learn about Odyssey's incredible mission. Find out where Odyssey is right now. Then check out the great photos of Mars.

NASA

http://www.nasa.gov/
The National Aeronautics and Space Administration home page lists past, present, and future space missions. You can learn about each American astronaut who has gone into space. There are also great photographs of the Moon, the space shuttle, and celestial bodies.

INDEX

ABOUT THE AUTHOR

Mark Beyer is an editor and writer living outside of New York City.